GOODBYE HORSES

Also by Nathaniel G. Moore

Bowlbrawl (Conundrum Press, 2005)
Let's Pretend We Never Met (Pedlar Press, 2007)
(co-editor) *Toronto Noir* (Akashic Books, 2008)
Wrong Bar (Tightrope Books, 2009)
Pastels Are Pretty Much The Polar Opposite of Chalk (DC Books, 2009)
Savage (Anvil Press, 2013)
Jettison (Anvil Press, 2016)

GOODBYE HORSES

Nathaniel G. Moore

Mansfield Press

Library and Archives Canada Cataloguing in Publication

Moore, Nathaniel G., author
Goodbye horses / Nathaniel G. Moore.

Poems.
ISBN 978-1-77126-184-5 (softcover)

1. Catullus, Gaius Valerius--Poetry. I. Title.

PS8626.O595G66 2018 C811'.6 C2018-902736-3

Cover Image: Shutterstock
Author Photo: Finnian Hastings
Design: Denis De Klerck
Editor for the press: Amber McMillan

The publication of *Goodbye Horses* has been generously supported by the Canada Council for the Arts and the Ontario Arts Council.

ONTARIO ARTS COUNCIL
CONSEIL DES ARTS DE L'ONTARIO
an Ontario government agency
un organisme du gouvernement de l'Ontario

Canada Council for the Arts Conseil des arts du Canada

Mansfield Press Inc.
25 Mansfield Avenue, Toronto, Ontario, Canada M6J 2A9
Publisher: Denis De Klerck
www.mansfieldpress.net

For Amber

TABLE OF CONTENTS

I dreamed that you bewitched me into bed
And sung me moon-struck, kissed me quite insane.
(I think I made you up inside my head).

—*Mad Girl's Love Song*, Sylvia Plath

HOLD ONTO YOUR FRIENDS

Nobody ever chooses the already unfortunate
as objects of his loyal friendship.

—Lucan

THE DEDICATION: TO CORNELIUS

To whom do I send
this fresh bait book
of sex soot,
just floating ghastly as snow?
To you, Cornelius:
since you have gone
through customs,
considered my inky truffles
worth their caloric weight
even then, when
you felt yourself
lonely for *explicit italics,*
dared to explain these pages.
So swell chum,
take this little book
and tuck it in your coat,
whatever colour it is,
and cherish its mirth:
virginal as fresh brassica,
lend it fast, for more days
than one.

Or simply—

Here it is for everyone
or none,
polished all the same.
But firstly to you, Cornelius:
Superfriend read as you have read
With tender hooks and eyes.
Pass on to those equally full of it:
piss and affection for days!

SWEET SWELLING GIRL

Ipsithilla, don't make this love a language difficult, opaque
and strange. Let us aim for cute, pretty, lifting, and sweet;
Ipsithilla my tart, she heaves well, the late morning a ghost
as my delicacy opens for me; outstretched. Her body
will parade a paradise you'll soon see off this page. I'll find
myself at her door knocking, breathing through the wood,
promising her nine successive interludes of whimper, of limbs
wet, of joyous tears, of moaning sound streams and me
and my fashion: a tunic no more; my body now only flesh.
Clothless and knocking, heart and soul and foot and tooth
so push aside, a string of sausages fresh from the Botularius
or tomacula from a swelling Popina; invite me now. I'm here.
Entreaty me this after-lunch desire; do not comment on my cloak
a material blur without comfort, of little or no consequence.

SEVEN LINES HENDECASYLLABIC: TO CICERO

The sole communication between you and I
exists in these seven lines of verse.
You speak so well; better than all who tread
in rain or sun or future Roman weather.
And I give you great thanks from me, the worst
of all poets to the greatest of orators,
forever defending all our soft lives.

A WORD PLEASE: TO CORNIFICIUS

He's ill, Cornificius, your Catullus,
  infirma, heart punched by Hercules
and it's bad; worse and worse by the hour.
Where are you now friend
   for whom it's the least and easiest thing
to bring consolation with chatter?

I'm cross with you. So much
  for my friendship?
Even a little might comfort me,
I'm sadder than a plate
  of Simonides's tears.

INVITATION: TO FABULLUS

Wouldn't you like to get away?
Could you imagine a week?
The fruits will dance on our plates!
In just a few days my dear Fabullus,
bring a carriage full of produce
and a pretty girl for dessert and wine—
kale crisps, avocado, chains, whips
and all your ample laughter.

WHAT A BOOK: TO CALVUS THE POET

When my eyes are homes for small fish,
I will still be reading your great book, Calvus.
Now what did I do and what did I say
to be so badly cursed with pen pals?
Let the gods send ill-luck to that client
who sent you so many wretches.
But if, as I guess, Sulla the grammarian
gave you this new and inventive gift,
that's no harm to me, it's good and fine
that your efforts aren't all wasted.
Scholarly gods, graze us with your presence.
Read a mortal's long-lasting book
that you sent, duh, to your Catullus,
so he might immediately drown
on the optimum day in the Saturnalia.
No you won't get away with this gift.
Now when I want to read more from the drip
I'll slither by those treacherous copyists bookstalls,
I'll drink down Caesius, Aquinus, Suffenus—
all of the poisonous ones. I'll repay you for this
snuffing out. Meanwhile, farewell. Take yourself
off, there, whence your unlucky feet brought you,
cursed vocation, cursed first, we are all
slim-volumed, the worst of poets.

BACK FROM SPAIN: TO VERANIUS

Veranius, the pal I think of first in a line of thousands,
I'm so hopeful and joy-blessed to hear you're back
at your mother's place with your brothers, too,
safely at the table telling us about Spanish places
the sun has kissed you so hard and for so long;
O who but me is this happy?

THERE SPEAKS A TRUE FRIEND

If you can take in kind the pleasures of civility
when speaking of a true friend and knowing
no god has interjected witchcraft, nor rigged the day
to deceive us all, you'll be just fine in this hapless state.
Yes, Catullus, you will wear this love as a badge of honour
because what true kindness can be shared in words of faith
or act of worth? Well, all this and more was given
to some wretched heart; all that's lost turns blind and ill,
so siphon all that brings you joy and please stop
all this vexing grief and end it quietly
as the doting gods look wistfully upon us;
I beg them to treat me well, find me at my most fearful,
my most honestly appointed and give me strength
as strong as my belief in their rugged power and love.

MY VOICE FALTERS, MY TONGUE IS BROKEN

Never does Nature say one thing and Wisdom another.

—Juvenal

HARD DAY

Pretty, coy and fickle,
but still Juventius, you are loved,
sluttish boy.

I count phantom kisses
all the while you need not lie
of where you lay.

Honey-eyed doe,
melting at the hem of wastrels,
your mouth and heart:
twin forms of depravity.

LAKESHORE

Paper, I order
you politely
now to firmly
say to Cecilius,
no to simply say,
to just say
to that soft poet,
that friend of mine,
to leave Lake Como,
run on water from here
to Verona and abandon
his lame town,
the boring shore.
There are certain
thoughts I want him
to hear from his friend.
So, if he's wise,
he'll eat up the road
though some lovely girl
calls to him,
asks his return,
clasping both hands
round his neck
and begging delay.

Who, if the truth's
been told to me now
love's him with violent
desire. Since the moment
she read his unfinished
Lady of Dindymus,
the poor little thing
has been naked
to the core, dripping
pear juice and crying
his name. I forgive you,
blonde more learned

than a Sapphic Muse:
it's truly lovely,
your fervor is unfinished
business, tender tenero
of his friend and of me.
Let's avoid negative
peers here in Verona
and tap along
to this eventual
phalaecean metre:
start your march, leave
the Larian lakeshore.

FLAVIUS' GIRL: TO FLAVIUS

Flavius, unless your delights
were tasteless and mirage,
you missed a poached eggs brunch
seaside and waves crashing shyly.
Surely you're in love with some mime
who doodles whoredom: you're ashamed
to undress it. Now, walking heavy on eggshells
is one thing, but you don't seem to be idle-
handed at night, we can hear the horns blasting
from your bedroom and the night air fills
with your familiar brand
            of penny-soaked cologne
            the kind ditch diggers save up for—

But miming death to hide away your new love
does nothing for you, Flavius. We know
you live somehow, breaking bread
with a fair-headed, motor-mouthed doll
you bend over a tree branch to kiss.
How slyly you've got her good or drab, tell us.

I want to name you and your love lexically
with ash from this unfortunately close
            burning bush.

AFTER SAPPHO'S φαίνεταί μοι

He seems to measure up to a god,
all the gods really,
sitting opposed to you
often and again gazing,
listening to you intently

          and the speaking,
your laughter steals my energy—
for I did not inspire it—
my *enallage* tongue,
my limbs, ears, eyes,
forced by wild flame numb
as I tremble.
I hear only incessant humming.

Leisure, Catullus, suits you not;
it pains you, it pelts you
with desire beyond measure,
the type that made rulers crumble
and happy towns poor.

EVERY MOON IS ATROCIOUS AND EVERY SUN BITTER

When you are lonely, become your own crowd.

—Tibullus

NECROPICNIC

Rufa of Bononia, wife of Menenius,
    blowing hard her friend Rufulus,
who do I speak of you ask?
I'm sure you've seen her frequently,
    necrophiliac in training,
prancing disgustingly at midnight,
proudly half nude,
    wildly grabbing the meat
baking on the pyre
    or chasing dinner rolls
wheeling past the fire
only to be comically wacked
    on her dirty head with a rake
by a half-shaved undertaker slave.

AVE ATQUE VALE

Spanning countries, bodies and seas;
multiple rivers, I'm here with my heart
beneath a shield reading the epitaph,
now polished. Still, brother, devastating
in perpetual abstention from joy,
stolen thoughtlessly from life
you tumble softly into death's elegies
like birds seize the daze. Brother
crudely sacrificed for reasons I know
not but accept, a pyre consumed with tears
so elegant, forever a stream in my mind.

BEYOND THE GRAVE: TO GAIUS LICINIUS CALVUS

If, from our grief, anything
    can reach past
death's shadow cast in the deaf grave,

we give up pain, revive our lost loves,
    and weep over vanished pals.
Accept Quintilia's forgettable death.

She is pleased to be loved by you, Calvus,
    but now wipe all this away
and make it forgotten because it is like

she never left us; especially you Calvus,
    your love remains
even now in sad removal.

GOODBYE HORSES

A horse never runs so fast as when he has
other horses to catch up and outpace.

—Ovid

1.

You get the feeling, emotionally realistic,
that you met your love seconds before,
no, hours before, weeks before the Trojan War—
he was Protesilaus and you were Laodamia—
but since you were wed, and since the war,
sorry love, friendship—*my Lesbia, my brother—*
and since now you know the marriage ended,
not from lack of love but from death,
and now you, perhaps, hoping in a sad way,
you are feeling as awful as the widow Laodamia,
lacerating her cheeks, mourning Protesilaus,
that you, in this moment, spent by ruined measures,
send me this terse text, horseback, curled in tears,
forged from a cursed, shipwrecked life.

2.

Forged from a cursed, shipwrecked life,
tussled by the sea: can we see him return
from death's sickly shack, for whom
heavenly Venus provides no aftercare,
alone in a kissless bed? I'm your friend
in love and know your tone; I wrote this poem,
so therefore please forgive me if the gifts
don't arrive; grief has taken me by surprise.
I do not have a great mountain of writings,
I am at my family home in Verona, weeping
into my adolescent hand-me-downs:
a densely fragrant toga—formerly worn
by my brother who was so recently,
unhappily subtracted from this life.

3.

Unhappily subtracted from this life,
brother, you were dying, death's eff-
luvium, neither kind nor sad poem
has been sent, but will be sent—and softly
right to you, pinned to you somehow—
in spirited flight it will find you, seek
you in the rough. I feel I do not have
the right to feel, a lack of zeal permits
me this entitlement. I wouldn't want
you thinking that I'm doing this venting,
this tear-letting out of anger—I swear
I am not, and years from now, many
thousands, it may not matter. For now,
make this roll of papyrus speak.

4.

Make this roll of papyrus speak,
make good on its assessment when I too
am no longer young but gone: a simile
might modify my tears or Allius' *auxilium.*
Be wary of lexical maladjustment,
O Manius, such grief does it bring. Gods,
are you there? I am being forthcoming,
I produce testament unasked, without gelding.
I can't mute myself as my own life witness.
Goddesses, how truly, in fact, with sacrifice
Allius Manius has helped me, however you try
in vain to forget. White chalk may flee in rain,
yet the love I felt those days remains.

5.

Yet the love I felt those days remains,
none can deny, not even two-faced Venus
who watched me now burning like Etna's
Sicilian core, or the gushing hot orange
gates of Mount Oeta, those swelling sulphur
springs still wet in memory, sequestered
to the sloping valley, nourished in regret.
Who knows the wounded skies above, who
says it's too late, perforated from the Earth,
this conformation finds sweet comfort
while some, tormented by dark channels
of wind so grateful I am to Allius Manius:
he leant me his house for Lesbia to go inside,
deep into her heart and so long ago now.

6.

Deep into her heart, so long ago now
the worn floor massaged her feet
and she took me—did I tell you friend,
about blond Cupid sporting a yellow tunic
made of soft saffron, running around
Lesbia's taut legs? Which Catullus
satisfies her? Certainly not just one,
who was loving and attended sequential
trysts now a memory ash; even Juno,
the greatest of all the goddesses,
often digests her own burning resentment
at her husband's wrongdoing,
reporting to the all-lusting Jupiter.
Laodamia learned how the hungry feed.

7.

Laodamia learned how the hungry fed
her great-hearted Protesilaus, the first
to die; his step on Troad a broken sandal
tattered, its leather flecked in righteous
splatters of hollering love. The wicked
arrow from Hector, or Aeneas, Achates,
Cycnus or Euphorbus, his upright blood
tumbled on the coldest shore sand
where she lowered her husband's neck
before winter fell to the tune of a neigh
or whinny. Gorgeous the marriage was,
dearer to you than anything, and this
was taken from sweet Laodamia,
more thoroughbred than clotheshorse.

8.

More thoroughbred than clotheshorse,
the teenaged Helen was snagged by Theseus
Protesilaus' sheep and eaten in the night.
I think of my quarrelsome pigeon Lesbia,
who could never decide on her desire. I follow
a wider path now where my sadness cannot
cut through sudden rolls of this sunken valley;
I travel tirelessly in sick-hot weather, Laodamia
and I, knocked about like sailors at sea, tortured
and hurt, and love no more, our idle pleasures
whirled in a flood, your mind a catastrophic
stream, rushing past the swamp where Hercules
killed the Stymphalus' beast, transformed
into airless tears for 187 minutes. To this total,
the gods will add an embarrassment of gifts.

9.

The gods will add an embarrassment of gifts:
the impious vulture jaw, sculpted in morbid ridicule,
the snow-white pigeon rejoicing, pecking at kisses
heartlessly from the lips of love itself, from the tip
of what everything joyous was originated, the dramatic
sculpture of milk-white horses of Troy, gallivanting
strong, plus many more gifts, signed in the presence
of a distant relative dearer to me than I myself
could ever be. My life is at pace, is sweet with her,
alive. Our love no less deep than Hercules effortless
chasm in Acadia. I allude to many premature deaths
and do the same for love, with news of Paris our eyes
sparkle near the flaming torches, his willing arrow
springs unperturbed from the bedroom.

10.

Springing unperturbed from the bedroom:
Why do you attack love as if you were going
to strangle it? The war spoke around us,
the still-young Helen married to war,
the very-young Helen's abduction or seduction,
the fruitlet Helen dangled by Aphrodites
and the music they constantly played,
oppressed by fortune. Bite into calamity;
it is shameful for Catullus to be at Verona,
but I am here. Where better tarts' warm, sad
limbs livened up an otherwise abject couch,
my bookcases—the crooked one from Rome—
have followed me. It makes me sound callous:
I'd give you all you desire if I had the means.

11.

I'd give you all you desire if I had the means,
let not a spider who weaves her thin walls
ever spread her work in the deserted tears
for Allius. Remember tears, hot ones, contested
at Trinacrian rock, along the Malian water
at Oetean Thermopylae. Always tears on my face,
no other skill! Brother, brother in this poem,
along with Troy, dead and gone so long,
my face a lake, my cheeks a stream, my mouth
a whirlpool as my sobs fall on deaf ears.
Know as the lofty mountain knows, ignorant
and true, grief is never brief, but my brother's
death takes this from me. *Conquer or concede*
shouts blond Cupid in my nervous lap.

12.

Shouting, blond Cupid in my nervous
lap, Lesbia wanting too much and less,
enough is too much—*I repeat*—
One Catullus? Two Catullus? Three?
Or a thousand of Jupiter's kisses,
godly-smacked against her face,
against her behind and against her neck?
Of course with passion for her and for
those parts. *Stupid Cupid poking me.*
Tonight, glistening soft in a yellow tunic,
kindly made of Crocus Cultivé, you know,
Azafrán, and so Lesbia, nevertheless always
more and never satisfied with one Catullus.

13.

More and never satisfied with one Catullus,
ongoing are the frustrating trysts. Look
what I produce unasked; ask me and I won't
veer off truth's path, but tell you as honest
as the waters of Malis. Speaking of which,
even the gods will never silence me about Allius
and his help in my matters of love, no matter
how many house flies and spiders. Forget
his name, he who lent his home for Lesbia
and I, and remember the prayer to Allius' bride
hoping we had not cursed her fair marriage bed.
Because of my brother's death however,
so sudden and so sore, I cannot think about
the favour you did me, or its wondrous results.

14.

The favour you did me, its sensational results,
the gold the silver and brown tornado
eating eighty sailors, takes me from my thoughts
of Allius Manius. The prayers to Castor
and Pollux were submitted, and yes, Lesbia and I
loved that day, all day of days, her noisy sandal
in my mouth, cherishing the minutes like Laodamia
did until the flesh became memorialized
because clay became bronze, a limited statue,
because I am red-eyed and hard on myself,
on my brother-less life for my life with Lesbia
is like her sparrow is gone. We are all despised
it seems, known as third-rate crooners;
you get the feeling: emotionally realistic.

15.

You get the feeling, emotionally realistic,
forged from a cursed, shipwrecked life,
unhappily subtracted from *this* life,
to make this roll of papyrus speak.
Yet the love I felt those days remains,
deep into my heart; so long ago now
Laodamia learned how the hungry feed,
more thoroughbred than clotheshorse.
The gods will add an embarrassment of gifts,
springing unperturbed from the bedroom.
I'd give you all you desire if I had the means,
shouting, blond Cupid in my nervous lap,
more and never satisfied with one Catullus:
the favour you did me, its sensational results.

RANK

Any man can make mistakes
but only an idiot persists in his error.

—Cicero

Believe me, wise men don't say "I shall live to do that."
Tomorrow's life is too late; live today.

—Martial

NIGHT AND DAY

You know Gallus has those brothers, right?
One has a glorious son, one a spritely wife.
Gallus is such a cutie: why? Because he goes to bed
with all the them. Gallus is also a moron,
can't hack it as a hubbie. He tells his nephew
where to stick it during complex bouts of adultery.

COMMON PEOPLE: TO FURIUS

Furius, you have props for insides;
a place to come in and get dry.
A soul desiccated year-round.
Why wouldn't you be well and sane?
You've no pulse, no sinus phlegm,
no master plan or mucus membrane.
You make love to your daddy
and his sex slave; your pantry is bare
as your buttocks. Why go out to find
love when it's in such proximity!
You shit such a little amount,
your asshole seems brand new.

THE LAST WORD: TO GELLIUS

I've often been concentrating
   on just how I could send Callimachus's poems
so they'd soften you toward me,
so you'd not try to land your calumny spears
   toward my precious throat.
Now I see I've put the cart before the horse,
my good intentions such bright failures.

DEAR COMINIUS

If your hoary-haired spirit
is soiled by your impure ways,
by will of the people,
I have no doubt, for my part,
your tongue will go first.
The enemy of good will
will be cut out and fed
to eager vultures, your eyes
gouged out and swallowed
by black-throated ravens,
your intestines wasted by dogs
and the rest of your body,
choked back by wolverines.

LISTEN WITHOUT PREJUDICE

Your terse arrows hurt; they ride me well
Furius and Aurelius, you, who name yourselves
friends of Catullus. Whenever I may roam
India, the oceans east, my eyes away Hyrcanians,
Sacians or Parthian, my feet touching the multi-
mouthed Nile, I see the tiny waters of Gallic Rhine,
and the furthest fierce Britons. Tell my girl this:
Let her live and be gay with her enablers,
hold all three-hundred by their pubic hair,
take them for a walk over our fading days
and live and love rottenly, heartlessly; wear them
all out with one big hump; drag them up and down
the welted streets; let her never look for my true
faith further, she whose body crimes Rome nightly,
the last flower pulled with a hungry jaw.

NO POET: TO MENTULA

Mentula tries his hand at climbing the Parnassian ridge.
Crows caw—the Muses
                                        with farm tools crowd around.
Take turns tossing him back down.

STOP STEALING THE NAPKINS: TO ASINIUS MARRUCINUS

Stop Asinius Marrucinus,
even if you think you've heard
this one before—your manners
don't seek employment,
your stomach hunts for fast food
as your left hand makes the shape
of a magic wand. Your dinner jacket,
merlot coloured and scented.
Do you think that's witty?
You should believe Pollionus,
your brother, who wishes your thefts
could be fixed by money: he's a boy,
truly stuffed with sophisticated tools.
So I expect three hundred hell pics
or return my napkin, whose value
doesn't disturb me. It's only
a remembrance of my friends.
Fabullus and Veranius sent me
the posh mouth wiper to begin with,
coming all the way from Spain.

SUFFENUS

Hey Varus, silly Suffenus,
over-known to us all,
so well he must live
in our houses, perhaps under
the stairs. Yes, it's here
where he writes
his ten thousand poems,
new volumes, new roller ends,
new red bowties
for the polished parchment,
toxic garbage, childish gibberish
smothered in self-love.
When you read them,
that homely hipster Suffenus
turns into a pretty ditch digger:
so ultimately strange.
He's amazed by his own two-step,
hiccups and breathing.
It's been done. We've done it,
and do it still, but still,
something about Suffenus—
amplest supplies, dimmest results,
and my how I could go on.

GREEDO: TO AURELIUS

Aurelius, father of hungers,
you desire to push phallus

not just against these kind folks,
but whoever my friends are, too.

You hunt time with that prick,
not secretly, and at the same time

as you shoot your blasting mouth
with one, you try fettering another

to your prick in vain. You should
look out for interfering toga snakes.

So step off while you have shame,
or end up in an all-night burglary.

BLIND

Caesar,
I don't care
where you
place me,
in good
standing
or bad, nor
can I look
up past the sun
to see if you
have a face
at all.

ON A STUPID HUSBAND

O Colonia, who has rolling hills
winding on forever upward,
far from Tartarus's sad taverns
though you fear the useless law,

the burning forests will raise
the price of furniture as they tumble
with flame and lie in deep ash:
let a good chair be made from cinder,

dust and brine, to sit on in a game
of leap-frogging. Colonia, give me
that greatest gift, a good prawn.
I want a fellow-citizen of mine

to go summersault straight into
the deep from your rooftop bars,
on a night of rubbish when the blackest
sky is tarred. The man's totally skull,

knows no more than a two-year-old
chimp, asleep in its father's lice-pooled
arms. Some poor bride is in chains
and tears. We tire of passing figs,

eating grapes, discussing your weak
new love. We fill a Ligurian ditch
with fog and hearsay. Who knows
if your wife is real or phantom art.

Such is his prosaic nature, he who doesn't
see or hear, he who doesn't know
what day it is, or whether he is pet
or houseplant. Now I want to toss him,

Hercules style, from your crumbling
rooftop of happy hours and watch.
The mules will nudge his bloody shoes
with their useful noses.

DEAR RUFUS

Rufus, do not ever wonder
why the feminine thunder
never calls you back or ceases
flopping on your bed—yes,
you're a real bore, a bad cheat,
but a certain dirty trope
haunts your foul armpits.
It has become ritual, really,
with this thing, the beast within
your skin. Local legend has it
a farm goat dwells
beneath your shoulders.

LET'S PRETEND WE NEVER MET, RUFUS

You pretend friend to humanity,
humility beckons you, and, as history lends an ear,
you turn my guts into hate. If you had wanted to come
at me, man to man to discuss this, that would've been
all right but you've been hot-dogging and grand-standing.

You've got lust in your eyes
and dirty ice buried deep in your cemetery of a mind,
melting away, leaving a crude facsimile. I once called you
my friend. I've sipped from the poisonous air we share,
a terror now exists between us in the rude thermae.

PESARO PALLOR

Is that the best you can do, my loving
idiot Juventius? You choose the yellowing
Pesaro, dastardly pimp-tart of no class.

Rape apology rental agreement:
your new boyfriend is a dogmatic
piece of shit who fucks you now instead.

HEY LOOK, IT'S EGNATIUS!

As an animal cannot detect pain
until after the hunt, I too carry on,
falling from the bar down a few stairs.
The beautiful Spanish bartender
just ran out of Caesar mix; she looks
toward the broken step while I hold
my arm and she tells me someone
is fixing the stairs in the morning.
My arm is pickled in bruises, stinging.
The cook threw cold meat over a flame
as I slowly roll up my sleeve and eat
fast food and dress the flesh wound.

So a reminder to you, from me,
my good Egnatius. If you were a Sabine
or Tiburtine, a round Umbrian,
a chubby Etruscan, a snaggle-toothed
Lanuvian or from north of the Po,
if you were urbane, and I'll mention
my own Veronese, too, or whoever else
scrubs their teeth religiously, I'd still
not want you to smile all the time:
Now you're Spanish of Spain,
now you're a Celtiberian of Celtiberia,
now the gurgler morefull of piss.

DOCTUS POETA

May I write words more naked than flesh, stronger than bone,
more resilient than sinew, sensitive than nerve.

—Sappho

ATTIS AGAIN

Traversing great dark seas,
Attis, speedy catamaran,
sprinting impatiently toward
those woods in Phrygia
with soot on your foot.
Attis with frenzy of tingle,
Attis, poor romantic, doomed,
mutating in gender, in forest
and love, raw in the manic
world with a red-mouthed
chomp, castrating himself
for Cybele. Attis, you enter
a sexual anti-twilight and we
zone in on his screaming,
I'm all yours! A tiny tugging
boygirl, a human litany
of haunting memories! Attis,
ghosts, shamanistic ally,
s/he's expansive, a vapour
of lust and intrigue, post-
genital, ungentle, all balls
and circles, shapeshifter and rut
all at once. And the first violets
blossomed. *Now come along,*
walk now with me, worshippers
of Cybele, to the lovely bushes
of the deity; meet my doomed bride,
Pessinus. Attis, distracted
wallflower, who unmanned himself
moments ago: *First we take*
this mound, then Mount Sipylus,
Mount Coddinus, Phrygia.

CEASE FOLLY

Cease folly, Catullus.
Count what is lost as lost.
Rest, remainders, truth: the sun

circling her ass without you.

Catullus, brightly, nightly
be firm. Endure but never give
misery the right of way.

PHASELUS

What a hunk of junk
said a daft farm boy,
well, he might have said
something similar
of this boat described
before you, my friends.
It was the fastest floater
he might have continued,
praising its unrivaled
sea-foaming abilities
with no other vessel aflutter.
In any weather blown hard
by sail or the axis of oars!

The seductive Adriatic coast
won't deny it, the Cyclades
isles cannot lie, nor noble
Rhodes, nor Bosphorus,
nor the mordant bay
by the Black Sea, where,
before boat puberty,
she was a leafy tree: one
who on the tips of Cytorus,
was often tickled by wander-
lust sun. The yellow boat
laid rhythm in familiar octave,

backed up in song by Amastris,
a simple beat as she passed
Cytorus, boxwood full.
She says from the get-go
that she knew the groove:
imagined tiptoeing along
your grandmother's foot path,
from the river to home,
and she told the story
of how she dipped her oars

in your blood, carried on abroad
over so many heat strokes,
nude fish and wave breakers.
If the wind cried
from starboard or land,
or whether Jupiter
gave his boots a splash
in the deep end, in the rocky
shore, no promise to the salty
gods when she nudged along
midnight toward this lamped
lake. Now grandmother
has a cow to mend, a husband
to mourn, a home to tiny flies
named Castor and Pollux.

SIRMIO

Sirmio, set as jewel in pellucid fresh,
so nice to see you again.

I cannot fathom how I ever endured
the flat infinite plains of Bithynia, can you?

Exhausted, refined, refreshed, I will become.
My brain surrenders its crucial burdens,

finding the soft bed just as we dreamt, once.
Makes it worthwhile, no?

Hello my swell Sirmio, get happy, the master
is home. Be proud, each ripple,

each sunbeam stroking waves, the joys of home
explode in giddy laughter.

SYRIA EARFUL

C'est fort, I might have said, but said *effort,*
I'm sure. This dolt, now gone to Syria for a war or two

gives us peace, but once we start to talk like him,
to discuss his inept speaking ability, well, look now:

we're all mispronouncing everything. Hambush,
handbag, mother, brother, uncle, jungle, wolf, wool.

And once you've heard this story enough times,
you'll have heard the same thing more softly

and with *finesse,* a lilting tone to bring you to tears.
Oh, look who's back to bite off our ears.

LOWER EMOTIONAL CHARGE

Stop that game, don't waste your time

Phalaecian homoeoteleuton

No use to play hide and seek for a week

Assonances hole

For all your dreams are twins of mine

suffered synizesis

Don't think twice or count to ten

a pyrrhic via syntagms

Don't take advice, don't ask me when

Simple volitive raw

Just come my way, simply kiss me

necesse est

and say hands up, baby, hands up

a textual uncertainty

Haut les mains

obsolete or obsolescent in the ordinary language

Why don't the stars look at me?

several enclitics

It's a light summer night, no use panhandling

PRIMA MATERIA

Of such themes also sang the writings of wanton Catullus,
whose Lesbia is more famous even than Helen.

—Propertius

HOW MANY KISSES: TO LESBIA

Don't answer me Lesbia.
You ask how many kisses by you
would sop up the dream I own.
As many as the rivets on every vessel,
every jarring water line these ships
create, times a thousand thousand,
or as many as the night shares
single breaths. Breaths occurring
in between secret movements.
As many as your thick kisses
could kiss and more are too much
and enough for Catullus, as can be
counted by goddess and satellite,
never an evil tongue should siege us.

ADVICE: TO HIMSELF

Miser self, none the wiser well,
just plain ol' sad Catullus,
stop! You've heard this one
before, and now let it end.
Once, bright sun shone
out of our behinds. Now Lesbia,
cunnus, er, your vagina is a jokin'
some call a soft and warm *iocosus*
or *hocus pocus sans punchline*—
and so one of us becomes a puny
wretch, down to his last apple
core, discarded, disgusting:
she loves not! Your destiny,
Catullus, is in some wild orchard
and you, a still rock unkempt,
an undisturbed solo.

HER JERK-ASS MOVES

Lesbia drags me down
in front of her chub-hub.
It brings him great joy
well into the foul evening.
Jerk, don't you get it?
If she could forget me
completely and just sit there,
that would be one thing,
but because she whines,
because she squirms
as I swim in her brain,
those slanderous jabs
bring me out to prance.
She thinks of me with anger,
excitement, and the adjuration
toward our deepest love.

WOLF MOTHER

The Lesbia, this Lesbia,
the one and only ours,
to you I speak.

In rival alleys, Lesbia,
never alone now, loiters.

Hoisted up by, and tugging
on, Rome's wolfish
offspring.

TANTRIC WAVE

My babe says
there's no one else
she'd rather wed
than me,

even if Jupiter himself
popped the question.

So she says.
For what a woman says
to her chirping lover

should be written on air,
or tantric wave.

BLAZING TRUTHS

No one ever can say what
I've said, waiting for that final
moment, a true love strong
and far from wide, all the while
my regenerated desires trample
the orchards, you know this.

Never dry these emotional
tributaries we swim down,
or sicken at the sight of each
moonbeam, each gloom-sick—

My pledge bursts through
the skin, this longing thirst.
The truest part was truest to you,
so here it is: what I said
to you was the finest.

I meant it in the most ways.
My love for you never rests,
but remains natural.

PRETTY VACANT

Prissy Lesbius is a pretty
boy, why not?

Lesbia prefers him more
than you, your family too,

and yes, Catullus. Oh yes
we know Lesbuis

is her older brother, not quite
her lover, but still,

the pretty boy would sell
us all, Catullus too

if he finds three sufferers
of his taxing embrace.

HUMOURLESS

A beauty to some is Quintia.
To me she's snow white,
long-legged and well-crafted.
She's a big dish but no delight;
not a glimpse of humour
on her best Sunday dress.
Lesbia is totally awesome
beautifully so, dressed in
shades cooler and hotter
than the rest. She whispers, you
whimper: It's the one who deserts
you that you want for dessert.

TEARS ARE NOT ENOUGH

Lover, spare a thin, bright sesterius?
I'll pluck it in a wet meadow

to remind the world of your
goner bird. Lesbia's light bright,

whom now in dreams she lays with,
savors and nuzzles, whom greedily

she gives a little finger, often provoking
a sober bite. To play with something,

I suppose. Whenever my desire beacons,
weakness comes. A cold metallic plunk.

O dead thing, might I joy-fly with you
and ease the craze of summer sadness.

THE DEATH OF LESBIA'S SPARROW

My girl's house pet is dead, sparrow. Her firm
delight, whom she loved with wet brown eyes
for he was handsome and knew her well.
He never flapped from her warmth, but now
he goes across the river of dregs from which
some say no one returns. Now let evil sting you,
evil mirror of Orcus, that tenderize beauty:
you've stolen lovely from me. Now, sour efforts,
my girl's eyes are swarmed red, unforgiving.

Occasion stares my way as if my activities
were entirely more vivid, my feathers fluorescent,
beak hard and crisp through the smoky breakfast
air. Then death came for me, and as was done before,
by thousands before, in no original act. Fluttering
in the bedroom like treading water, eventually
muscles will seize up, cease. The bird world
was swatted, swallowed. The art I sketched with tiny
talons had no intention nor permanence, and is gone
now where things are gone without heartbeat.

LET'S LIVE AND LOVE: TO LESBIA

Let us lust, present-tense,
my emotional Lesbia,
let us love all: the head, the liver
too. We are unrefined,
we are high-minded and oral.
May they discover us entombed
in a kiss, lips next to lips lit
by moon. Give me an ocean-worth
of kisses wet, a hundred more on land.
In the sunshine of your love, hand
over another thousand, and another
hundred and sixteen, the funk
of forty-thousand years, and when
we've counted up that kissy tab,
no enamel may cast a wrong
finish by knowing what number
this kiss here is.

THE GLORY OF LOVE

My mind is threadbare
on your subject, Lesbia, ruined
by our ignoble encounters,
the power of your devotion.

I can't wish you a good day,
though you are good,
and if you were not so,
I'd still want you.

A PRAYER: TO LESBIA

I remember now, near the fabulous, false
decorative tree as she shredded the buttered toast
in a fit against her soft lips and when closed,
these lips formed a temporary pink rose
and her nipples slept well under an incandescent
gown, which by now phantoms on a floor
somewhere, beneath all my derangement.

The outlaw garment, once removed, revealed
a corporeal estate as if she was preparing to feed,
pantomiming a dirty balance of sustenance
and eros. Now my inadequacy rises, now
my duress circulates and the potion of hope
vanishes, the vanity of defeat and predictive flaws
self-propel: I am the designer, but cannot feel
the plan for all I feel is love.

MUSIC FROM THE EDGE OF HEAVEN

Catullus scarcely has a decent poem,
I don't think Sappho's Ode a good example.

—Lord Byron, *Don Juan*, Canto I, XLII

In a recent essay in *Classical Receptions Journal*, Dr. Katherine Wasdin discusses the late Kathy Acker and her relationship with classical Greek and Latin authors in her landmark novel, *Blood and Guts in High School:* "The main character, Janey, first translates several poems of Propertius, switching her identification between the male author, who serves as model for desiring poet, and his beloved Cynthia, a female speaker. She then meets the ghost of Catullus, who leads her to her death; on the final page of the book is an unattributed version of Sappho fr. 16 V."

Wasdin suggests Acker's passion for dead poets such as Properitus[1], Catullus and Sappho come from how she viewed them in the canonical afterlife of literature, rebels who battled "against traditional norms and, like her, [were] deeply interested in questions of gender, love, and power." One could say that Acker has an intertextual relationship with these writers to offer "a programmatic statement about gender relations and literature." Wasdin touches on how Catullus affects the author, in a near-mantra like caveat, that I very much identify with: "As a symbol of Acker's compositional methods, Catullus is both an inspiration and a deadly temptation."

I first tripped over poetry as a teenager. I had spent about half a decade in mourning my early romantic burglary year (1987-88) and my perceived eleven months of high-octane popularity at age thirteen. Poetry was passionate and had a directness I didn't know could be obtained by writing things down. At the cusp of my second decade, poetry was the true filter; however crudely I was constructing my voice, this voice was the loudest. I had a healthy outlet for my fantasies.

These days, as I walk through the valley of my shadowy cerebral cortex, I can pinpoint the exact moment I first read the name Catullus and his lexical attachment to the woman he loved and her infinite capacity for sexual inspiration. Spiritual inspiration too, as Catullus was not just a wind-up penis, hopping from bed to bed. It was a rainy evening in November of 1995 and I had stepped into a used bookstore near the university to find a tattered book with a title like *Roman Civilization*, and as I read from it in snacking portions over the next several weeks, found myself returning to the short passages describing who Catullus was, how he was different from the traditional poets of the Late Republic, how he disguised his secret love, Clodia Metelli, by calling her Lesbia, a nod of the proverbial hat to the Isle of Lesbos and Sappho, whom she admired. Two months later, as if I'd conjured up some lost love, I found a new book in Coles at the Eaton's Centre in Toronto which I bought for a couple of dollars: *From Bed to Bed* was an abridged version of James Michie's *The Poems of Catullus*. At the indoor fountain, adjacent to Orange Julius, I began to pour over Michie's versions of Catullus' greatest hits. His druggy words had taken hold of my 21-year-old mind.

Thinking of Catullus as a musical band (which, technically it is in New Jersey) the young poet started out as a cover band for Sappho, and much like the Beatles, stopped covering the hits of a previous generation and started working on his own material. Like many in his day, the influence of Greek mythology and poetry is entirely obvious. And as Ezra Pound said in *The Egoist* in 1917, "The Greeks might be hard put to find a better poet among themselves than is their disciple Catullus."

Through Catullus, from the first day until now, I find myself both creator and excavator. My archeology of Catullus is necessary for me to maintain passion. For example, I've recently discovered that Lesbia's true identity wasn't known until she was identified by the north African writer, Lucius Apuleius, who wrote the Latin novel *The Golden Ass* in the second-century. When Ovid wrote *Trista* a few decades after Catullus's death, he did not know who she was, simply that she had existed:

Often did salacious Catullus sing
about his lover, hiding her as Lesbia

Their private love was not enough. He advertised it
all the time, proclaiming his adultery.

Martial, a Spanish poet from first-century Rome, was by all evidence a complete Catullus obsessive, always trying to outdo Catullus with carnival barker-type hyperbole, wanting to be the poet who answered "how many kisses," for example. The seventeenth-century brought Ben Jonson and Catullus together, while the following century ushered in William Carlos Williams, Wordsworth, Lord Byron, Christopher Marlowe, Walter Savage Landor, Thomas Moore, Leigh Hunt and Charles Lamb, so meek and tame in his translation, one critic called his work "absolute murder[2]."

After nine thousand days he still inspires me. One could easily spend a quarter-day trolling journals, online forums, used books, PDFs of texts culled from the nineteenth through to the twenty-first century and find convivial Catullus chatter, chards of intellectual inquiry such as the "ethnic phonetic play in Catullus[3]" and other esoteric fodder which makes my Catullus cup runneth over with joy daily.

As the years piled on, I would get word of new (new to me) versions of Catullus lingering on the page. In the fall of 2001, my poetry best friend, Tavis E. Triance wrote to me saying, "You need to go to the library and find Louis Zukofsky's Catullus. I don't know what it's like, but Zukofsky has some amazing stuff; the Catullus bit you can figure out." While I saw the Zukofskys's radical phonic/sonic transliteration of Catullus as an inventive and important addition to his post-mortem, it didn't inspire me; their renderings leaned too heavily on the experimental and didn't offer any breathing room into the lyric. Reproducing the assumed sound of Catullus' Latin into English above the literal meaning, seemed to me to be an overextended gimmick.

Many have dug up Catullus' bones. One can nearly hear a ghostly librarian softly say, "Is there a Francis Peacock Simpson[4] in the audience? Your book was just checked out of the library," and Ann Carson seems to have covered the inventive aspects of Catullus' work like a rock star. The feeling I get is this: to not complete these poems would render me flat, starved of mirth, and leave me with a digest of apocalyptic portents, highly unhappy, unable to dance.

Twelve years after first reading his name in that paperback, I published *Let's Pretend We Never Met* (Pedlar Press, 2007), a poetry-prose hybrid (now out of print, but email me I'll send you the PDF) dealing with my obsession with the dead Latin bard up to that point. While I moved onto other projects, dozens of Microsoft Word files with "Catullus" in the title remained entombed in my hard drives and email archives, gaining age and their own unique vintage.

"Catullus intended to offend, which is why he is so loved and hated," said Carl Sesar, who first published a collection of Catullus in 1974. I've often wondered, however, if Catullus had not died so young, would he have segregated his more disgusting poems or perhaps placed them on their own away from his more beloved ones? In the same interview, Sesar stated, "No matter how nasty or repellent he gets in certain of his poems, he manages to do it with such great impact and such style you're forced to swallow them as art." It's all about context, I guess. When I asked about this stream of thought in an interview I conducted with Daisy Dunn, the author of *Catullus' Bedspread: The Life of Rome's Most Erotic Poet*, she said, "There were aspects of Catullus which were very difficult to write about from an emotional perspective. How does someone in the twenty-first century talk about Catullus's jokes about rape, for instance?[5]"

His many translations into English have made him feel like a contemporary poet. In her book *Catullus*, Julia Haig Gaisser writes, "Catullus is the most accessible of the ancient poets. His poems convey an emotional immediacy and urgency that claim reader's sympathy." Catullus wrote about things both highly accessible and abdominally personal; he was an obsessive poet who wrote of the beautiful and abject. Camille Paglia, in her book *Sexual Personae*, wrote, "Catullus, like Baudelaire, savors imagery of squalor and filth. His moral assumptions remain those of republican Rome which he jovially pollutes with degeneration and disease. His poetry is a torch-lit descent into a gloomy underworld where we survey the contamination and collapse of Roman personae."

What is it about Catullus that makes me keep coming back to him like a favourite vampire, knowing full well he's about to appear in your bedroom from a lightning storm-lit terrace and parse familiar phraseology in a family cadence? It's the mystery, the obsessive academia, the ethereal moments such as when I sat in a movie theatre a decade ago watching a cowboy film about Jesse James,[6] (which takes place in the 1880s, filmed in Calgary, starring Brad Pitt and Casey Affleck) and a supporting actor/cowboy cocksmith named Dick Liddel of all names, quotes Catullus to demonstrate his bravado as it relates to fellow cowboy and hired hand Ed Miller's trouble with a prostitute whose words he mistook for love:

Ed Miller: Yeah, sure, she been with other people. But the kinds of things she said to me, people just don't say unless they really mean it.

Dick Liddil: "My love said she would marry only me, and Jove himself could not make her care, for what women say to lovers, you'll agree, one writes on running water, or on air."

After quoting the infamous marriage poem about Jove/Jupiter, Ed Miller, giddy, suggests they use these lines in a note to the woman, and, like a classic Catullus punchline, derogatory, satirical and harsh, Dick Liddil replies, "Naw. Poetry don't work on whores." The truth is Ph.D candidates continue their witchcraft on Catullus; podcasts on his subject are being recorded and shared online; terrible and terribly acted high school-level Catullus-based history projects go up on YouTube every year; new biographies, essays and emo children of the internet are quoting the poet on Twitter as they guide their paper hearts through this cruel world.

When I read a Leonard Cohen poem from forty years ago, I see the lineage to Catullus' own sad state of romantic affairs. Take "I Heard of a Man" from *Let Us Compare Mythologies*. Perhaps it's a unique reaction I've forced myself to see, but I hear Catullus' own "Poem 51," which begins with, "To me that man seems like a god..." a poem of quasi-acceptance, of frustration, longing, anger and spiritual unrest. When I hear a six-week-old pop song sung by a twenty-nine-year-old pop diva (male or female), I think of cultural theories that examine Catullus' riffs on Lesbia as a literary construct, while the person she is in reality, lives free of his literary garrison, his own poetical and abject constraints of her person. She is a character who, through the ages has been slut-shamed, nearly deified, and perhaps aptly described by Camille Paglia as "cynical Lesbia, adulteress and dominatrix...vampiristically draining the strength of all." Hardly the type of personal information one would use on an online dating profile. Lesbia is a character, but Clodia Metelli gallops faster past this sketch of a woman.

When I see a tearful sibling interviewed on the news about his dead brother, I think of Catullus' lasting "Poem 101" (*Ave atque Vale*—for all time, hail and farewell), the tribute to his dead brother; a poem so lasting in fact, it's an online sample poem to read at a funeral. But my job is not to fill in the blanks for you, sing you a Catullus jingle or tell you anything more about Catullus than what I wish to say. He existed long before me, and will exist, outside of me, long after you read this book.

It's been nearly a quarter century of Catullus thump, thump, thumping at my door, a Jacob Marley-type haunting, but now I'm more interested in honouring him than pretending to be him or pretending to be haunted by him. These versions of his poems written now, in my forty-third year, are that attempt to understand, to know and reflect him as best I can.

While a new crop of Catullus fans may rise and begin their own version of my entry into Catullan obsession (oblivion), I'm still jogging on pace for whatever goal Jupiter has dared me to accomplish in my lifetime. And I know who will be waiting for me at the finish line, eating a tofu sparrow sandwich.

---

[1] Propertius said that Catullus made Lesbia more famous than Helen of Troy.

[2] *A Cockney Catullus: The Reception of Catullus in Romantic Britain*, 1795-1821 by Henry Stead

[3] "Ignatius's Dental Fricatives" (Catullus 39.20) by Joshua T. Katz, *Classical Philology*, Vol. 95. No. 3 (2000)

[4] *Select Poems of Catullus* by Gaius Valerius Catullus, Francis Peacock Simpson (1879)

[5] Interview, *Verbicide* (2017)

[6] *The Assassination of Jesse James by the Coward Robert Ford*, film (2007)

ACKNOWLEDGEMENTS

Some of these poems appeared previously in *Grain, Matrix, New Poetry, Touch the Donkey, PRISM International*, and *Canadian Literature.*

Thanks to all the editors, especially Lucas Crawford, rob mclennan and George Murray. My superlative gratitude extends to Denis De Klerck for his enthusiasm for the dead man and my own work. Books I am grateful for having been written include: *The Poems of Catullus* by Peter Green, *Clodia Metelli: The Tribune's Sister* by Marilyn B. Skinner and the highly amusing *A Cockney Catullus: The Reception of Catullus in Romantic Britain, 1795-1821* by Henry Stead. Thanks continue to Dr. Katherine Wasdin for her permission to quote from her essay in *Classical Receptions Journal*, and Dr. Maxine Lewis for her encouragement. Thanks forever to Amber McMillan for the exquisite edits and our daughter Finnian for her amo/ love and support.

Photo credit: Finnian Hastings

Nathaniel G. Moore is the author of seven books including *Savage*, winner of the 2014 ReLit Award for Best Novel. His poetry and fiction have appeared in literary magazines across Canada and the US. Born and raised in Toronto, Moore currently lives in Fredericton, New Brunswick with his wife and daughter.

Selected Titles From Mansfield Press

POETRY
Leanne Averbach, *Fever*
Tara Azzopardi, *Last Stop, Lonesome Town*
Nelson Ball, *In This Thin Rain*
Nelson Ball, *Some Mornings*
Nelson Ball, *Chewing Water*
Nelson Ball, *Walking*
Gary Barwin, *Moon Baboon Canoe*
Samantha Bernstein, *Spit on the Devil*
George Bowering, *Teeth: Poems 2006–2011*
Stephen Brockwell, *All of Us Reticent, Here, Together*
Stephen Brockwell, *Complete Surprising Fragments of Improbable Books*
Alice Burdick, *Book of Short Sentences*
Alice Burdick, *Flutter*
Alice Burdick, *Holler*
Sarah Burgoyne, *Saint Twin*
Jason Camlot, *What The World Said*
Pino Coluccio, *First Comes Love*
Marie-Ève Comtois, *My Planet of Kites*
Dani Couture, *YAW*
Gary Michael Dault, *The Milk of Birds*
Frank Davey, *Poems Suitable to Current Material Conditions*
Adebe DeRango-Adem, *The Unmooring*
Pier Giorgio Di Cicco, *Dead Men of the Fifties*
Pier Giorgio Di Cicco, *My Life Without Me*
Pier Giorgio Di Cicco, *The Visible World*
Pier Giorgio Di Cicco, *Wishipedia*
Christopher Doda, *Aesthetics Lesson*
Christopher Doda, *Glutton for Punishment*
Glen Downie, *Monkey Soap*
Rishma Dunlop, *Lover Through Departure: New and Selected Poems*
Rishma Dunlop & Priscila Uppal, eds., *Red Silk: An Anthology of South Asian Women Poets*
Puneet Dutt, *The Better Monsters*
Laura Farina, *Some Talk of Being Human*
Jaime Forsythe, *Sympathy Loophole*
Eva HD, *Rotten Perfect Mouth*
Eva HD, *Shiner*
Jason Heroux, *Hard Work Cheering Up Sad Machines*
Jason Heroux, *Natural Capital*
John B. Lee, *In the Terrible Weather of Guns*
Jeanette Lynes, *The Aging Cheerleader's Alphabet*
David W. McFadden, *Abnormal Brain Sonnets*
David W. McFadden, *Be Calm, Honey*
David W. McFadden, *Shouting Your Name Down the Well: Tankas and Haiku*
David W. McFadden, *What's the Score?*
Kathryn Mockler, *The Purpose Pitch*
Leigh Nash, *Goodbye, Ukulele*
Lillian Necakov, *The Bone Broker*
Lillian Necakov, *Hooligans*
Peter Norman, *At the Gates of the Theme Park*
Peter Norman, *Water Damage*
Natasha Nuhanovic, *Stray Dog Embassy*
Catherine Owen & Joe Rosenblatt, *Dog*
Corrado Paina, *Cinematic Taxi*
Corrado Paina, *The Dowry of Education*
Nick Papaxanthos, *Love Me Tender*
Branka Petrovic, *Mechanics of a Gaze*
Shannon Quinn, *Nightlight for Children of Insomniacs*
Stuart Ross et al., *Our Days in Vaudeville*
Jim Smith, *Back Off, Assassin! New and Selected Poems*
Jim Smith, *Happy Birthday, Nicanor Parra*
Robert Earl Stewart, *Campfire Radio Rhapsody*
Robert Earl Stewart, *Something Burned along the Southern Border*
Meaghan Strimas, *Yes Or Nope*
Carey Toane, *The Crystal Palace*
Aaron Tucker, *Punchlines*
Priscila Uppal, *Sabotage*
Priscila Uppal, *Summer Sport: Poems*
Priscila Uppal, *Winter Sport: Poems*
Steve Venright, *Floors of Enduring Beauty*
Brian Wickers, *Stations of the Lost*
Tara-Michelle Ziniuk, *Whatever, Iceberg*

FICTION
Marianne Apostolides, *The Lucky Child*
Sarah Dearing, *The Art of Sufficient Conclusions*
Salvatore Difalco, *Mean Season*
Paula Eisenstein, *Flip Turn*
Sara Heinonen, *Dear Leaves, I Miss You All*
Jason Heroux, *Amusement Park of Constant Sorrow*
Kasia Jaronczyk, *Lemons*
Christine Miscione, *Carafola*
Marko Sijan, *Mongrel*
Tom Walmsley, *Dog Eat Rat*
Corinne Wasilewski, *Live from the Underground*

NON-FICTION
George Bowering, *How I Wrote Certain of My Books*
Mark Cirilo, *Pizza Cultura*
Pier Giorgio Di Cicco, *Municipal Mind: Manifestos for the Creative City*
Amy Lavender Harris, *Imagining Toronto*
David W. McFadden, *Mother Died Last Summer*
Deborah Verginella, ed., *Buon Appetito Toronto!*

For a complete list of Mansfield Press titles, please visit mansfieldpress.net